Thai Cookbook

Extremely Easy Chicken, Beef, Seafood, Lamb and Vegetable Recipes

Disclaimer

The author has tried to be an authentic source of the information provided in this report. However, the author does not oppose the additional information available over the internet. The objective of providing different Thai recipes is to enable readers to try these delicious recipes at home. The recipes included in this book cannot be compared with the preparation methods of the same provided in other books. All readers can seek further help through additional sources of information. Also, the pictures in the book may appear different from the actual recipe.

Ignoring any of the guidelines or not following each step of the preparation method of Thai dishes may not give you the exact result. Therefore, the author is not responsible for such negligence.

Thai cuisine represents a fascinating combination of culture, art, and food. It blends natural ingredients with traditional Southeast Asian herbs to create a fine aroma which is simply irresistible. While Thai food is known for its spicy flavor, it also offers a wide range of herb infused and mild entrées.

It might seem a little complicated in the beginning; however, by following a step by step guide, you can master this cuisine in no time. From intricate curries to mouthwatering sauces and dips, this book is an easy guide for all Thai food lovers.

If you are on a special diet plan, you need not to worry about extra calories, sugar or cholesterol that you might intake; because with our nutritional guide section, you can have complete control over your diet. This will not only allow you to choose more easily, but will help you compare two food choices.

What does this book have for you?

- Top 50 most recognized and versatile Thai cuisines
- Easy to understand procedure
- Chef's most recommended recipes
- Ingredients that are readily available
- Vital nutritional facts about every recipe
- Divided into 5 broad categories

Whether you're trying Thai cooking for the first time, or just want quick recipes to add variety to the menu, you'll find exactly what you're looking for in this book. So, go ahead and show off your culinary skills to friends, family, and loved ones!

Contents

Thai Chicken

Thai Style Chicken Breasts

Serves 4

This delicious meal is an excellent option for special occasions and get to gathers. Instead of chicken breast, you can also use thighs, or boneless chunks. These lusciously moist chicken pieces go well with steamed rice!

Cooking time

Total Time: 35 minutes

Prep Time: 10 minutes

Cook Time: 25 minutes

Nutritional value

Calories: 387.1
Cholesterol: 75.5mg
Carbohydrates: 44.4g
Protein: 29.5g
Fat: 10.1g

Ingredients

Brown sugar 1/2 cup

Chopped garlic 2 tablespoons

Crushed red pepper flakes 1/8 teaspoon

Fish sauce 1 teaspoon or anchovy paste 1 teaspoon (optional)

Flour 1/2 cup

Flour to taste

Grated fresh gingerroot 2 1/2 tablespoons

Olive oil 2 tablespoons

Salt and pepper for seasoning

Snap pea 1 cup sugar (mange tout)

Soy sauce 4 tablespoons

Thinly pounded skinless and boneless chicken breasts 4

White wine vinegar 1/2 cup

Method

Dredge chicken pieces in flour and add salt and pepper to taste

In a skillet, bring olive oil to heat and add chicken. Cook the chicken pieces until both sides have turned golden brown. Take the browned chicken out of the skillet, and store in a low heated oven to keep it warm.

In the same pan, sauté gingerroot, garlic, and red pepper flakes until it turns light brown. Then add brown sugar, fish sauce, soy sauce, and vinegar and simmer carefully. After bringing the mixture to boil, reduce the heat and keep stirring until the sauce becomes a little dense.

After transferring the chicken in a serving dish, pour the mixture evenly onto the chicken.

Just before serving, sprinkle the diagonally shredded sugar snap peas on the chicken and serve hot.

Thai Chicken with Fried Rice and Basil

Serves 2

The stimulating aroma of basil and other Thai ingredients makes this the chef's favorite!

Cooking Time

Total Time: 20 minutes

Prep Time: 10 minutes

Cook Time: 10 minutes

Nutritional value

Calories: 538.7
Cholesterol: 72.5mg
Carbohydrates: 63.5g
Protein: 30.4g
Fat: 16.9g

Ingredients

Vegetable Oil 2 tablespoons

Boneless skinless chicken breasts, 8 ounces (cut into bite-size pieces)

Chopped fresh cilantro 1 tablespoon

Chopped shallots 2 tablespoons

Cold cooked rice 2 cups

Fish Sauce 1 tablespoon

Fresh Thai Red Chili Pepper (chopped) 1 tablespoon

Minced Garlic 3 cloves

Soy Sauce 1 tablespoon

Sugar 1 tablespoon

Thai or regular basil 1/3 cup

Method

In a wok, stir-fry garlic until golden. Then add chicken and chilies and continue frying until chicken is completely cooked. Now add rice, fish sauce, sugar, and soy sauce and mix gently while frying. When everything is well mixed, add basil leaves, cilantro, and shallots; cook for another few minutes, and serve.

Thai Chicken with Rice Noodles and Asparagus

Serves 4

This delicious and easy to make meal is sure to delight your taste buds from the very first bite. It is not much spicy; however, you can adjust the spices according to your own taste. You can even replace the meat with vegetables because this sauce works well with everything.

Cooking Time

Total Time: 40 minutes

Prep Time: 20 minutes

Cook Time: 20 minutes

Nutritional value

Calories: 435.6
Cholesterol: 72.8mg
Carbohydrates: 55.1g
Protein: 28.9g
Fat: 10.2g

Ingredients

Asparagus spear, preferably diced into 2 inch pieces 1/2 lb

Skinless and boneless chicken (thinly sliced) 1 lb

Brown Sugar 1 tbsp

Chili-garlic sauce 1 tbsp

Salt 1/2 tsp OR Fish Sauce 1 tbsp

Minced garlic cloves 6

Oil 2 tablespoons

Rice noodles 1/2 lb

Soy Sauce 2 tablespoons

Method

Soak noodles in hot water for about 15 to 20 minutes. Use medium heat and stir-fry garlic in a large skillet until it turns golden. Add chicken and fish sauce or salt and cook until done. Add chili pepper sauce, brown sugar, and soy sauce keep mixing until sugar is completely dissolved. Stir-fry drained noodles with asparagus until firm yet tender. Serve your delicious meal and enjoy!

Thai Coconut Chicken Curry

Serves 4

This recipe is a fantastic combination of creamy coconut milk and delicious curry paste. To add taste and texture, serve it with Jasmine rice or top it with green onions.

Cooking Time

Total Time: 35 minutes

Prep Time: 15 minutes

Cook Time: 20 minutes

Nutritional value

Calories: 491.1
Cholesterol: 0.0mg
Carbohydrates: 78.9
Protein: 2.0g
Fat: 20.4g

Ingredients

Boneless skinless cubed chicken breasts, 2 cups

Brown Sugar 1 teaspoon

Caned coconut milk, unsweetened, 1 (14 ounce)

Chopped green onion 1

Fish Sauce 2 teaspoons

Fresh Ginger, minced 1 teaspoon

Garlic clove, minced 1

Pineapple chunks 20 ounce

red curry paste 1 -2 teaspoon (1 for medium and 2 for hot flavor)

Salt 1 teaspoon

Stalk lemongrass, (first outer layer removed cut in half) 1

Vegetable oil 1 tablespoon

Water 1/3 cup

Method

In a large wok, fry the garlic in oil until its light brown. Add the ginger, curry, ginger and the cream of coconut milk and whisk regularly. Now add the remaining coconut milk and all other ingredients except the pineapple and chicken. Keep whisking and bring the mixture to a slow boil. Then discard the lemongrass and add pineapple and chicken. Keep cooking until chicken is cooked from the inside.

Spicy Thai Chicken Nuggets with Peanut

Serves 4

Spicy peanut bake can transform simple chicken nuggets into a delicate Thai cuisine. This is perfect to be served as an appetizer, snack, or even as an entrée.

Cooking Time

Total Time: 16 minutes

Prep Time: 10 minutes

Cook Time: 6 minutes

Nutritional value

Calories: 220
Cholesterol: 30mg
Carbohydrates: 16g
Protein: 11g
Fat: 12g

Ingredients

Box spicy peanut bake 1-3.5 ounce

Chicken breast tenders 1 1/2 lbs (about 1 1/2 inch long pieces)

Sweet Red Chili Sauce (Optional)

Vegetable oil or spray

Method

Brush over or spray the oil over baking sheet and foil. Pour Spicy Peanut Bake and chicken into a plastic bag until the tenders are evenly coated. Carefully lay pieces on the foil and broil for 6 minutes or until tenders are completely cooked. Serve with your favorite dipping sauce. Our favorite is sweet red chili sauce. It should ideally produce 30 pieces, however the amount of serving may differ depending on the size chicken pieces.

Thai Chicken Pizza with Peanut Sauce

Serves 2

Treat your senses with this mouthwatering Thai chicken pizza. With traditional Thai ingredients, give the local California pizza a delightful touch. With this easy to prepare recipe, turn your family dinner into a fiesta! Its sauce tastes amazing with boiled noodles. So save the left over sauce for the next day's supper.

Cooking Time

Total Time: 40 minutes

Prep Time: 15 minutes

Cook Time: 25 minutes

Nutritional value

Calories: 1353.2
Cholesterol: 181.1mg
Carbohydrates: 63.4g
Protein: 79.1g
Fat: 90.8g

Ingredients

The following ingredients will yield two pizzas.

Spicy peanut sauce

Honey 1 tablespoon

Red wine vinegar 2 teaspoons

Minced Ginger 2 teaspoons (Add more for a stronger taste)

Minced garlic cloves 2

Toasted sesame oil 2 tablespoons

Soy Sauce 2 teaspoons

Vietnamese chili sauce 1 teaspoon OR dried chili flakes 1 teaspoon

Oyster sauce 1 tablespoon

Water 2 tablespoons

Peanut butter 1/2 cup

Hoisin sauce 1/2 cup

Thai chicken pieces

Olive Oil 1 tablespoon

Boneless skinless chicken breasts 10 ounces (cut into 3/4 inch cubes)

For the pizza

Chopped fresh cilantro 2 tablespoons

Chopped roasted peanuts 2 tablespoons

Cornmeal or flour for handling

Pizza dough (readymade or homemade)

Scallions (diagonally cut) 4

Shredded carrot 1/4 cup

Shredded mozzarella cheese 2 cups

White bean sprouts 1/2 cup

Method

Sauce
In a pan, combine all sauce ingredients, and cook over medium heat. While mixing, bring the mixture to a boil, and divide the sauce into two equal portions, as it will be used for both Pizza and Chicken.

Thai Chicken
Over medium heat, cook the chicken in olive oil for about 6 to 7 minutes. Then refrigerate the chicken until its chilled. Coat the chilled chicken pieces with sauce and again put it in the refrigerator.

Pizza
With a large spoon or a butter knife spread the remaining sauce evenly over the pizza dough. Make sure that the sauce stays within the rim. Then coat the sauce with ¾-cup cheese. Now dust over half of the chicken pieces over the cheese along with carrots, bean sprouts, and green onions. Finish the toppings by sprinkling the remaining ¼ cup cheese and chopped peanuts on the pizza. Carefully transfer pizza into the oven and bake for about 9 to 12 minutes. The base should be crisp with bubbling cheese on the

top. When done, bring it out of the oven and dust the shopped cilantro over the hot cheese.

Barbequed Thai Chicken Kebabs

Serves 2

These scrumptious chicken kebabs are a perfect choice for any day, and any time. Whether you choose to barbeque it or grill it, its fine aroma, and creamy flavor is everyone's favorite. For added taste, marinade the chicken in coconut milk and curry paste for at least two hours. You can also add a spoonful yogurt to make it more healthy and moist. Better yet, get creative, and try it with green Thai curry sauce for a milder taste.

Cooking Time

Total Time: 20 minutes

Prep Time: 15 minutes

Cook Time: 5 minutes

Nutritional value

Calories: 251
Cholesterol: 85mg
Carbohydrates: 10g
Protein: 36g
Fat: 11g

Ingredients

Boneless and skinless chicken breasts, 2 (cut into large pieces)

Coconut milk 2 tablespoon

Courgette (also known as Zucchini), cut into chunks, 1

Deseeded red pepper chopped, 1

Lime, 1 (to serve)

Red onion, diced in shape of wedges, 1

Traditional Thai red curry paste 2 tablespoon

Method

Heat a grill pan to high or fire up the barbeque. Mix chicken in coconut milk and curry paste until each piece of meat is evenly coated in mixture. Now alternately thread the chicken pieces and vegetables onto the skewers. Cook the skewers for 5-8 minutes until it's done and charred. Make sure you keep turning the skewers for a well-done chicken. Serve with plain white rice. Squeeze lemon for added flavor.

Mexican Style Thai Chicken

Serves 5

This casserole is a sensational fusion of Asian and Mexican taste. Feel free to alter the taste according to your own choice by increasing or decreasing the spices. Instead of chicken legs, you may also use diced chicken breast. Invite your native friends over, and show your creativity.

Cooking Time

Total Time: 1 hour 25 minutes

Prep Time: 30 minutes

Cook Time: 55 minutes

Nutritional value

Calories: 251
Cholesterol: 85mg
Carbohydrates: 10g
Protein: 36g
Fat: 11g

Ingredients

Can coconut milk 1 (14 ounce)

Chicken Pieces, 8 legs

Chopped onion, 1

Coriander 1 teaspoon

Cumin 1teaspoon

Flour 1 ½ cups

Fresh minced garlic 2 tablespoons

Grated lime zest 1 -2 teaspoons

Hot chili sauce 1-tablespoon hot chili sauce

Minced fresh ginger 2 teaspoons

Peanut butter 2 tablespoons

Salt and pepper (For seasoning, as per your taste)

Soy sauce 2 tablespoons

Vegetable Oil 5 -6 tablespoons

Method

Heat oil in a skillet and set oven to 350 degrees. In a bowl, coat the chicken legs in a mixture of flour with a bit of salt and pepper. Fry the lightly coated chicken for about 8 minutes each side and shift it on a casserole dish.

Now add in garlic and onion, and sauté it until tender brown. Then add cumin, ginger, coriander, chili sauce, peanut butter, and soy sauce and stir for another 2 minutes. Now add in coconut milk and further cook for 2 more minutes.

Next, pour the sauce over the chicken, cover it with foil, and bake for 25 minutes. Again, uncover the chicken and continue baking for another 30 minutes. Enjoy your meal with herby rice. Do not forget to add in the grated lime zest at the time of serving for additional flavor.

Thai Chicken Roasted Drumsticks

Serves 4

Are you bored of the traditional drumsticks? See how Thai ingredients can enhance its flavor and aroma.

Cooking Time

Total Time: 55 minutes

Prep Time: 15 minutes

Cook Time: 40 minutes

Nutritional value

Calories: 246
Cholesterol: 66mg
Carbohydrates: 5g
Protein: 31g
Fat: 14g

Ingredients

Crushed garlic, 1 clove

Grated orange zest, 1

Orange juice 2 tablespoon

Skin removed chicken drumsticks, 8

Sweet Chili Sauce 2 tablespoon

Thai red curry paste 1 tablespoon

Method

Preheat oven between 200C to 180C, and line the baking tray with foil. Mix orange juice, zest, chili sauce, curry paste, garlic, and ¼ tsp salt vigorously, and coat the chicken in the mixture. Place the chicken in baking tray, and roast for approximately 40 minutes. Serve hot and enjoy!

Chicken in Thai Green Curry

Serves 4

This no fuss recipe is big on taste!

Cooking Time

Total Time: 55 minutes

Prep Time: 35 minutes

Cook Time: 20 minutes

Nutritional value

Calories: 487
Cholesterol: 40.2mg
Carbohydrates: 55g
Protein: 35g
Fat: 26g

Ingredients

Curry Paste

Basil leaves (as per individual's own taste)

Black pepper ¼ teaspoons

Chopped hot green chilies, 3 (include the seeds)

Chopped shallots, 2

Coriander, 20g (stalks and leaves separated)

Crushed Kaffir lime leaves 1 teaspoon

Finely chopped lemongrass, 1

Fresh root ginger, 1cm piece (finely chopped)

Garlic cloves minced, 2

Grounded cumin and coriander ½ teaspoon each

Limejuice 1 tbsp

Sunflower oil 1 tsp

The Curry

Can coconut milk 14 ounce (preferably reduced fat)

Fish sauce 2 teaspoon

Green beans (halved lengthways) 100g

Light Muscovado or Granulated palm sugar ½ tsp

Lime leaves, 4 (freeze-dried)

Mange touts 100g (thinly sliced lengthways)

Skinless chicken breasts 3 boneless, (450g/1lb total weight), cut into bite-size pieces

Sunflower oil 1 tablespoon

For Serving

Boiled Thai fragrant rice, 250g

Finely shredded spring onions, 2

Lime wedges

Method

To make curry paste: Blend coriander, garlic, lemongrass, ginger, and shallots in a food processor. Then add chilies, three quarters of the coriander leaves, basil, ground cumin, lime leaves and limejuice, coriander, and pepper; and further pulse for a moment. Add oil in the mixture and set it aside.

For curry: Stir-fry the curry paste for about 2 minutes followed by adding 2/3 coconut milk. Cook until its form a think texture.

Add the chicken and cook until the meat is no longer pink. Then pour the rest of the coconut milk, sugar, and fish sauce and cook to form a creamy texture. Lastly, add in the lime leaves and fry for another 5 minutes.

Meanwhile, steam the beans and mange tout and beans for a few minutes. Serve the curry with fragrant Thai rice. Place the shredded spring onion and lime wedges at corners of the serving dish.

Thai Beef

Beef Strips with Thai Green Curry

Serves 4

This Thai beef cuisine gets its unique flavors as a result of blending many exotic ingredients. We want to ensure that you get the most from your Thai food experience. Whether you are looking for gluten-free foods, or have a peanut allergy, our dietary and allergy chart provides valuable information for all of our products.

Cooking Time

Total Time: 30 minutes

Prep Time: 14 minutes

Cook Time: 15 minutes

Nutritional value

Calories: 410
Cholesterol: 75mg
Carbohydrates: 17g
Protein: 30g
Fat: 24g

Ingredients

Beef sirloin steak, 1 lb, or 453.5gm (cut into thin strips)

Brown sugar 1 tablespoon

Can Coconut Milk 1-13.5 ounce

Chopped onion, 1

Fish Sauce 2 tablespoons

Fresh basil leaves, 1 cup (roughly chopped)

Frozen peas 1 cup

Green Curry Paste 1 tablespoon

Jasmine Rice or Rice Noodles (optional)

Oil 1 tablespoon

Tomatoes (quartered) 2 medium

Methods

In a large skillet, bring oil to heat. Quickly cook the steak place it aside. Now in the same pan, add. Coconut milk and let it boil. Then while stirring, put in the curry paste and cook until well mixed. After that, add fish sauce, onion, and sugar and stir-fry another 3 minutes. When the onions are translucent, add the tomatoes, peas, basil, and cooked beef. When ready, serve with rice noodles or jasmine rice.

Thai Pad Grilled Steak

Serves 4

Pad Thai Sauce makes both the marinade and the finishing sauce for this delicious dinner salad.

Cooking Time

Total Time: 2 hours, 23 minutes

Prep Time: 2 hours (for marinade)

Cook Time: 23 minutes

Nutritional value

Calories: 450
Cholesterol: 110mg
Carbohydrates: 37g
Protein: 38g
Fat: 13g

Ingredients

Garlic Chili Pepper Sauce 2 tablespoons

Fish Sauce 1 tablespoon

Mixed salad greens 8 cups

Brown sugar 2/3 cup

Rice vinegar 2/3 cup

Flank steak 1.5 pounds or 860.4gm

Pad Thai Sauce 1-3.25 ounce

Method

In a bowl, mix Pad Thai Sauce, Garlic Chili Pepper Sauce sugar, Fish sauce, vinegar, and sugar. This should make a mixture of about 1 3/4 cups. Poke the steak with a sharp knife or fork before marinating. Using 1 cup of dressing, marinate the steak in a refrigerator. After marinating, take out the mixture and boil it for 5 minutes. Preheat grill before placing the steak on the grill pan. Cook both the sides with equal timing. People who prefer medium rare will have to cook for a lesser time than the ones who like it well done. Toss the salad in the remaining mixture and place the thinly sliced steaks over it. Drizzle the entire serving with cooked mixture and serve hot!

Fried Thai Beef

Serves 4

Cooking Time
Total Time: 25 minutes

Prep Time: 15 minutes

Cook Time: 10 minutes

Nutritional value
Calories: 399.3
Cholesterol: 75.9mg
Carbohydrates: 20.2g
Protein: 25.8g
Fat: 24.3g

Ingredients

2 green bell peppers (cored and seeded) cut into 1/2 inch squares

Beef stock 3/4 cup

Brown sugar 1 tablespoon

Canned baby corn, 1 (drained)

Cornstarch 1 tablespoon mixed with 2 tablespoons of water

Fish sauce 2 tablespoons

Fresh gingerroot, 1 inch (minced)

Garlic cloves, 2 (minced)

Lean sirloin steaks, 1 lb (partially frozen)

Oyster sauce 2 tablespoons

Plain steamed rice

Shiitake mushrooms, 5 (stemmed and sliced)

Soy Sauce 2 tablespoons

Thai seeded red chili peppers, 4 -6 OR red pepper flakes 2 teaspoons (optional)

Vegetable oil 2 tablespoons

White onion, 1

Method

Slice the frozen beef thinly into 1"x2"strips. In a bowl, mix sugar, soy sauce, ginger, garlic, and beef. Let the meat marinate for at least 30 minutes at room temperature. Before cooking, take the meat out of the marinating mixture. In a wok, bring oil to heat and stir-fry the meat until browned. While frying, add green peppers, corn, onion, mushrooms, and Thai chilies. Then pour in the beef stock and marinade and cook for 5 to 6 minutes. In a separate pan, combine cornstarch, fish sauce, and oyster sauce; and stir-fry until a thick paste is formed. Pour the mixture onto the meat and serve with steamed rice.

Meatloaf with Thai Red Curry

Serves 6

With traditional red curry paste, there is no way you can go wrong with any meat, especially beef!

Cooking Time

Total Time: 25 minutes

Prep Time: 15 minutes

Cook Time: 10 minutes

Nutritional value

Calories: 380
Cholesterol: 135mg
Carbohydrates: 21g
Protein: 50g
Fat: 11g

Ingredients

Garlic powder 1 teaspoon

Chopped onion 1 cup

Egg, 1

Ground sirloin 1 lb or 453.6gm

Thai Red Curry Paste 1-1.75 ounce

Salt 1 1/2 teaspoons

Fresh cracked pepper 1/2 teaspoon

Ground chuck 1 1/2 lbs or 680.4gm

Garlic herb bread crumbs 1/2 cup

Chopped carrot 1/2 cup

Glaze

Brown sugar 2 tablespoons

Ketchup 1/2 cup

Thai Garlic Chili Pepper Sauce 1 tablespoon

Method

Oil a baking dish and preheat oven to 350°F. In a large bowl, add red curry paste, garlic powder, salt, pepper, and egg and whisk until well mixed. Then add in chunks of ground sirloin and chuck into the mixture. Separately blend carrots and onions in a food processor and pulse for a minute. Pour it over the meat along with breadcrumbs. Mix, and press it evenly into the baking dish. Prepare the glaze by blending brown sugar, garlic chili pepper sauce, and ketchup and pout it over the dish. Now bake for about 1 hour and 15 minutes. Let it rest for at least 10 minutes before serving.

Thai Beef Steak with Red Wine and Sirloin Tips

Serves 2

This recipe is a divine combination of exotic red wine, delicate Thai ingredients, and the goodness of fresh juicy meat. Try this once, and you will never have to get a steak take away.

Cooking Time

Total Time: 3 hours, 20 minutes

Prep Time: 10 minutes plus 3 hours (marinade)

Cook Time: 10 minutes

Nutritional value

Calories: 280
Cholesterol: 0mg
Carbohydrates: 43g
Protein: 40g
Fat: 0g

Ingredients

Brown sugar 2 tablespoons

Limejuice 2 tablespoons

Worcestershire Sauce 2 tablespoons

Fish Sauce 1 tablespoon

Sirloin tips 1 1/2 lbs

Red wine 1/2 cup

Garlic Chili Pepper Sauce 1/4 cup

Method

Carefully whisk and mix garlic chili pepper sauce, limejuice, red wine, brown sugar, Fish sauce, and Worcestershire Sauce until sugar is dissolved and a smooth mixture is formed. Pour the steak in an airtight jar or a zip-lock along with the marinade and refrigerate it for 3 hours. Remove the steak at least an hour before cooking or grilling. Preheat the grill, and cook the marinade for approximately 6 to 8 minutes. Then grill the steak to the desired level of doneness and serve with steamed vegetable of your choice.

Beef Satay with Thai Peanut Sauce

Serves 5

Its probably the first when you think about Thailand's street food! It is known for its tender soft beef with a juicy flavor of peanut sauce. If you are a fan of Thai food, there is no way you can miss this!

Cooking Time

Total Time: 2 hours, 15 minutes

Prep Time: 2 hours (to assemble and marinade)

Cook Time: 15 minutes

Nutritional value

Calories: 297
Cholesterol: 71mg
Carbohydrates: 47g
Protein: 43.9g
Fat: 15g

Ingredients

Coconut Milk 1-13.5 ounce

Fish Sauce 1 tablespoon

Flank steak (thinly sliced) 2 lbs or 907.2gm

Fresh limejuice 1 tablespoon

Lime wedges and chopped cilantro (optional)

Peanut Sauce Mix 1-3.5 ounce

Method

For best results, keep the skewers in water for at least 1-2 hours before cooking. Start by whisking coconut milk, limejuice, fish sauce, and peanut sauce mix in a large bowl. Put the steak slices in an air tight bag along with ½ cup of marinade mixture. Let it marinade for about 90 minutes.

Preheat grill and carefully place the threaded beef skewers on the pan. Cook it for about 5 minutes each side or until it has reached the right doneness level.

Pour remaining mixture in a skillet and bring it to boil. When it is thick enough, serve it as dip sauce with satays. Before serving, drizzle chopped cilantro and squeeze lime over the meat. Serve and enjoy hot!

Spicy Meatball in Red Thai Curry

Serves 4

Cooking Time

Total Time: 40 minutes

Prep Time: 20 minutes

Cook Time: 20 minutes

Nutritional value

Calories: 371
Carbohydrates: 4g
Protein: 31g
Fat: 26g
Saturates: 13g
Sugar: 3g

Ingredients

Bamboo shoots 225g drained

Basil 20g

Canned coconut milk 400ml

Egg, 1

Fine green beans 140g (trimmed)

Lean minced beef 500g (10% fat)

Limejuice – 1 small lemon

Red chilies, 2 (1 sliced and 1 chopped)

Rice noodles or basmati rice (to serve)

Thai red curry paste 1-1½ tablespoon (adjust the spices according personal taste)

thumb-size piece ginger, grated

Vegetable or sunflower oil, 1 tablespoon

Method

Put the minced meat in a bowl along with ginger, egg, and chopped chilies. After seasoning it generously, mix it well and shape the mixture into meatballs.

Now fry the meatballs in a non-stick pan until they are brown. Place the meatballs on a separate plate and start preparing the curry by adding curry paste, coconut milk and ½ can of water. Keep stirring until it takes form of a smooth sauce.

Return the meatballs back into the pan followed by adding beans and bamboo shoots. Simmer for 5 minutes or until meatballs are completely cooked and beans are tender. When serving, add basil and squeeze lemon over the curry. It tastes best with noodles or rice.

Coconut Thai Beef

Serves 2

Cooking Time

Total Time: 20 minutes

Prep Time: 10 minutes

Cook Time: 10 minutes

Nutritional value

Calories: 846
Carbohydrates: 64g
Protein: 36g
Fat: 48g
Saturates: 29g
Sugar: 18g

Ingredients

Beef steak 250g (rump can also be used)

Canned coconut cream 160ml

Coriander leaves ½ small pack

Crispy onions 2 tablespoons

Green beans 200g

Jasmine rice 300g pack (cooked)

Limejuice ½ lemon

Red Chili, 1 (thinly sliced)

Soft brown sugar 1 tablespoon

Thai green curry paste 2 tablespoon

Vegetable oil 2 tablespoon

Method

Rub 1 tablespoon of red curry paste over the steak. Heat oil in a pan and cook steak for 3 minutes each side or cook according to your desired doneness level. Now transfer it to another plate and keep it covered. Start preparing the sauce by pouring the remaining curry paste along with sugar, lime zest, coconut cream, chili, and sugar. Cook until it starts bubbling and it's thickened.

Meanwhile, in another pan, boil the beans for about 4 minutes, then drain. Now cut the beef into strips and add it in the sauce prepared. Serve it with hot rice and garnish the curry with coriander leaves, coconut dressing, and beans. Enjoy hot!

Thai Beef in Pita with Coriander and Red Peppers

Serves 4

Cooking Time

Total Time: 25 minutes

Prep Time: 10 minutes

Cook Time: 15 minutes

Nutritional value

Calories: 501.8
Carbohydrates: 42.9g
Cholesterol: 73.7mg
Protein: 33.1g
Fat: 21.8g
Sugar: 5g

Ingredients

Cilantro ½ cup

Fresh Ginger, 2 tablespoons (minced)

Garlic cloves, 3 minced

Green onions, 2 thinly sliced (also keep the green tops to garnish)

Lean ground beef 1 lb

Limejuice, 1 lemon

Peanut butter 3 tablespoons

Pita Pockets, 4

Red bell peppers, 2 (thinly sliced and seeded)

Red pepper flakes, 1 teaspoon (or less according to your taste)

Romaine lettuce leaf

Sesame oil 1 tablespoon

Soy Sauce 2 tablespoons

Method

Crumble the beef and cook over medium heat until it has browned. Now add peppers, garlic, red peppers, and ginger into the skillet and stir until peppers are tender and crisp.

In a separate bowl, whisk together cilantro, peanut butter, soy sauce, sesame oil, and lime juice. Now mix it into the pepper mixture and beef.

Cut pitas in two halves and line it lettuce leave. Fill each half with an adequate amount of meat mixture. Garnish it with green onions and serve.

Spicy Thai Ground Beef in Traditional Red Sauce

Serves 4

The recipe will introduce you a delicious new way to cook ground beef. Red curry can be used to make it even spicier. Children usually do not like minced meat; however, in this case, they will be happy to have it as snack also. Try using the meat in sandwiches – you will love it!

Cooking Time

Total Time: 20 minutes

Prep Time: 10 minutes

Cook Time: 10 minutes

Nutritional value

Calories: 425.4
Carbohydrates: 50.4g
Cholesterol: 73.7mg
Protein: 27.4g
Fat: 11.7g
Sugar: 7g

Ingredients

Asian fish sauce, 1 tablespoon

Brown sugar, 1 tablespoon

Cooking spray

Fresh limejuice 1 ½ teaspoons

Grated lime rind, ¼ teaspoon

Lean ground beef 1 lb

Low fat coconut milk, ½ cup

Minced garlic, 1 teaspoon

Red curry paste, 1 teaspoon

Short grain white rice 3 cups (cooked)

Thinly sliced leek, 1 cup

Tomato sauce, 1 cup

Method

Coat the pan with cooking spray and heat it over medium heat. First, sauté leek for 5 minutes, and then put garlic and cook for another three minutes. Now add beef and stir until it's brown. When it's completely cooked, stir in the tomato sauce and curry paste. Once the liquid is evaporated; add coconut milk, brown sugar, grated lime rind, limejuice, and fish sauce milk for about 3 minutes. Once it's thick and creamy, serve with hot rice!

Thai Seafood

Thai Fillet Fish with Oyster Sauce

Serves 8

Cooking Time

Total Time: 1 hour

Prep Time: 30 minutes

Cook Time: 30 minutes

Nutritional value

Calories: 164
Carbohydrates: 11.9g
Cholesterol: 60mg
Protein: 13g
Fat: 6.9g

Ingredients

All-purpose flour, ½ cup

Boneless fish fillet (cubed), 1 pound

Brown sugar, 1 teaspoon

Chopped fresh cilantro, ¼ cup

Egg, 1

Fish sauce, 1 tablespoon

Oil for frying

Oyster sauce 2, tablespoons

Sliced green onions, 4

Sweet chili sauce, 2 tablespoons

Method

Combine fish, oyster sauce, ½-cup flour, fish sauce, sweet chili sauce, cilantro, brown sugar, egg, and green onions in a food processor and pulse until well mixed. Refrigerate the mixture for 20 minutes before shaping it into patties. Dust the pieces with flour. Now in a large skillet, deep-fry the fish cakes until golden brown. Make sure you keep turning sides so that it's completely cooked.

Thai Tilapia with Lime and Coconut

Serves 4

Loaded with flavor, this dish is perfect for celebration dinner and other events where presentation matters a lot! The rich sauce over plain rice taste as good as it looks.

Nutritional value

Calories: 373.5
Carbohydrates: 44.1
Cholesterol: 85mg
Protein: 38.8g
Fat: 4.6g

Cooking Time

Total Time: 1 hour

Prep Time: 30 minutes

Cook Time: 30 minutes

Ingredients

Brown sugar, 1 tablespoon

Chopped fresh cilantro, 2 tablespoons

Chopped green onion, 1 cup

Cooked basmati rice, 3

Curry powder, 1 teaspoon

Ground cumin, ½ teaspoon

Lime, 1 (cut into 4 wedges)

Low fat coconut milk, 1 or 14 ounce

Low sodium soy sauce 4 teaspoons

Minced fresh ginger, 2 teaspoons

Minced garlic cloves, 2

Red bell pepper, 1 cup (finely chopped)

Red curry paste, 2 teaspoons

Salt ½ teaspoon

Sesame oil, 1 teaspoon

Tilapia fillets, 4 or 6 ounce

Method

Preheat broiler.

In a large pan, bring ½-teaspoon oil to heat. Cook garlic and ginger for about a minute and then add onions and peppers. After a minute, add curry paste, cumin, and curry powder and again cook for 2 minutes. Now pour in soy sauce, coconut milk, ¼ teaspoon salt, and sugar; and simmer slowly (do not boil). Then take the pan off the stove and stir in cilantro.

Separately, brush the fish fillet with ½-teaspoon oil and sprinkle over ¼-teaspoon salt. Place it over a cooking spray coated baking sheet. You can also use parchment paper.

In a preheated broiler, broil it for approximately 7 to 8 minutes. Check with a fork if fish is thoroughly cooked. Pour some sauce and serve the fillet with rice and lime.

Thai Salmon Bites with Lime

Serves 6

(About 40 Salmon Bites)

These delicate bites of salmon are extra yummy when dipped in our Peanut Lime Sauce.

Cooking Time
Total Time: 35 minutes

Prep Time: 25 minutes

Cook Time: 10 minutes

Nutritional value
Calories: 210
Carbohydrates: 7g
Cholesterol: 25mg
Protein: 12g

Ingredients

Coconut milk 1-13.5 ounce

Fresh squeezed lemon 3 tablespoons

Olive oil, 1 tablespoon

Peanut sauce, 1-3.5 ounce

Salt and pepper

Sesame seeds (black and white mixed) 6 tablespoons

Skinless salmon fillet 1 1/2 lbs

Tip: Black sesame seeds are widely available at Asian food stores

Method
Line a baking sheet with parchment or foil and heat the oven to 400°F.

In a bowl, add oil and salmon, salt, and black pepper and toss to coat thoroughly. Then dip one side of salmon on the sesame seeds and place the piece over the baking sheet, with dipped side downwards. Bake for about 8 to 10 minutes or until 8-10 cooked through.

Meanwhile, in a saucepan, add peanut sauce and coconut milk and cook until a thick paste is formed. Turn off the stove and mix in limejuice. Serve salmon bites with peanut-lime dip sauce.

Thai Shrimps with Peanut and Coconut

Serves 4

15 Appetizers

A tasty appetizer for a crowd, or enjoy it as a main course.

Cooking Time
Total Time: 15 minutes plus required marinade time

Prep Time: 10 minutes

Marinade: 3 to 4 hours

Cook Time: 5 minutes

Nutritional value
Calories: 690
Carbohydrates: 47g
Cholesterol: 455mg
Protein: 54g
Fat: 30g

Ingredients

Brown sugar ¼ cup

Chopped cilantro (optional)

Coconut milk 1-13.5 ounce

Extra large shrimps 3 lbs (peeled and deveined)

Freshly squeezed limejuice ¼ cup

Grated rind of lime, 1

Minced garlic cloves, 4

Minced ginger 1 tablespoon

Peanut sauce mix 1-3.5 ounce

Sweetened coconut flakes 1 cup

Method
In a bowl, whisk together; coconut Milk, peanut Sauce Mix, lime rind, coconut flakes,

brown sugar, ginger, limejuice, and garlic until well mixed. Then add shrimps and mix so that each piece is well coated with marinade. Preheat the grill or broiler, and grill or broil the shrimps until they are opaque. Serve with cilantro sprinkled over it.

Spicy Shrimps with Pepper and Garlic

Serves 2

With a strong tangling taste, it is the ultimate Thai delight. Feel free to replace shrimps with beef, chicken, or tofu.

Cooking Time

Total Time: 35 minutes

Prep Time: 25 minutes

Cook Time: 10 minutes

Nutritional value

Calories: 406
Carbohydrates: 12.1g
Cholesterol: 85mg
Protein: 12.3g
Fat: 35.6g

Ingredients

Chopped cilantro 1 tablespoon

Crushed red pepper flakes 2 teaspoons

Vegetable oil, 2 ½ tablespoons

Large shrimps (peeled and deveined) 8

Minced garlic 1 tablespoon

Shredded cabbage 1 cup

Sliced onions 2 tablespoons

Soy Sauce 1 tablespoon

Water ¼ cup

Method

In a skillet, heat 1 tablespoon of oil over medium heat and fry cabbage with 1 tablespoon of water for 30 minutes. Once done, place the cabbage on a serving dish.

Then heat the remaining 1 ½ tablespoon of oil and fry shrimp with garlic. Once golden brown, add water, onion, soy sauce, pepper, and cilantro to the pan and cook for 30 seconds. Pour the mixture over cabbage and serve hot!

Steamed Thai Crab Legs with Lemon Grass

Serves 4

The flavorsome steamed crab is Asian taste at its best. Dish up with favorite salad or spinach dressing.

Cooking Time

Total Time: 30 minutes

Prep Time: 15 minutes

Cook Time: 15 minutes

Nutritional value

Calories: 586
Carbohydrates: 5.3g
Cholesterol: 241mg
Protein: 89.1g
Fat: 20.7g

Ingredients

Vegetable oil 2 tablespoons

Pressed garlic clove, 3

Crushed gingerroot (1 inch)

Crushed lemon grass, 1 stalk

Fish sauce, 2 tablespoons

Oyster sauce 1 tablespoon

Salt and pepper to taste

Thawed cooked king crab legs, 2 pounds

Method

Heat oil in a large wok and cook ginger, lemon grass, and garlic until lightly browned. Then add in oyster sauce, fish sauce, and salt and pepper and sit to blend. Not put the crab legs, cover the wok, and cook for about 15 minutes. Serve hot!

Thai Prawns with Fried Rice and Peas

Serves 4

It's healthy, quick, and delicious! Serve it with fried rice to give it a flavorsome kick!

Cooking Time

Total Time: 20 minutes

Prep Time: 10 minutes

Cook Time: 10 minutes

Nutritional value

Calories: 287
Carbohydrates: 21g
Sugar: 3g
Protein: 22g
Fat: 12g

Ingredients

Chili sauce, (optional)

Cooked brown rice 300g OR uncooked rice 140g

Coriander, small bunch (chopped and leaves for serving)

Dark soy sauce, 1 tablespoon

Eggs, 4

Fish sauce, 1 tablespoon

Frozen peas 75g

Large peeled prawns, 250g

Red onion, 1 (sliced)

Sliced garlic cloves, 2

Sliced red chili, 1

Vegetable oil 2 tablespoons

Method

In a wok, heat 1 tablespoon of oil and fry garlic, onions, and chili for 2 to 3 minutes.

Then add prawn and cook for another 2 minutes. Now tip in the peas and cooked rice and keep tossing until steaming hot. Next, stir in fish sauce, soy sauce, and chopped coriander.

Meanwhile, in a separate pan, fry the eggs, and season them well. To serve, divide the rice and prawns into four equal portions, sprinkle the coriander leaves, and place a fried egg on each. Serve with chili sauce if you like it spicy.

Mint Thai Prawns with Lime

Serves 4

Cooking Time

Total Time: 1 hour

Prep Time: 45 minutes

Cook Time: 15 minutes

Nutritional value

Calories: 137
Protein: 16g
Fat: 9g

Ingredients

Chopped coriander leaves

Chopped garlic cloves, 4

Chopped lemon grass, 1 stem

Chopped red chili, 1 (seeded)

Chopped shallot, 1

Chopped Ginger root, 2½ cm piece

Handful of chopped fresh mint leaves

Limejuice and grated zest, 1 lime

Olive oil 100ml or 3½ ounce

Raw king prawns, 20

Method

In a bowl, combine all the chopped ingredients along with olive oil limejuice and zest; and let it rest for 30 minutes. Once the flavors are mingled in one another, add in the prawns and barbeque for 1 minute each side. Serve the prawns with egg friend rice for maximum taste.

Spicy Thai Tiger Prawn Cakes

Serves 4

Cooking Time

Total Time: 50 minutes

Prep Time: 30 minutes

Cook Time: 20 minutes

Nutritional value

Calories: 621
Protein: 33g
Fat: 29g
Carbohydrates: 61g

Ingredients

A pinch of sugar

Chopped coriander 3 tablespoons

Crushed garlic clove, 1

Egg noodles, 140g

Grated ginger root, 1 teaspoon

Grated zest, 1 lime and limejuice 1 tablespoon

Mengatout, 50g (thinly sliced lengthways)

Plain flour, 1-2 tablespoon (for dusting)

Red chilies, 2

Sesame oil 1 teaspoon

Shelled raw tiger prawns, 225g

Soy sauce 2 tablespoon

Spring onions, 3

Sunflower oil 3 tablespoons

Toasted sesame seeds 1 tablespoon

Method

In a food processor, add; prawns, 1 spring onion, 1 chili, sugar, lime zest, a pinch of sea salt, and coriander leaves and pulse to coarse a paste that has a think texture. Using floured hands, shape the mixture into 4 rounds, and fry the prawn cakes in 2 tablespoons of sunflower oil for 4 minutes each side.

Right after frying the prawns, put the noodles to boil. Meanwhile, in another pan, heat the remaining 1 tablespoon of sunflower oil and stir-fry ginger and garlic along with a seedless chopped chili for a minute. Then tip in the remaining spring onions and mangetout; and cook for another 2 minutes. Remove the pan from heat and pour in sesame oil, limejuice, and soy sauce.

Now add the drained noodles and prawn cakes into the stir-fry; sprinkle with coriander and toasted sesame seeds, and serve hot!

Steamed Thai Fish with Red Chilies

Serves 2

Nutritional value

Calories: 199
Protein: 29g
Fat: 7g
Carbohydrates: 7g

Cooking Time

Total Time: 30 minutes

Prep Time: 15 minutes

Cook Time: 15 minutes

Ingredients

Chopped garlic clove, 1

Red chili, 1 (seeded and finely chopped)

Limejuice and grated zest, 1 lime

Trout fillets, 2 (about 140g or 5 ounce each)

Soy sauce, 2 tablespoons

Baby pak choi, 3 (each quartered lengthways)

Ginger root, about an inch (peeled and chopped)

Method

Lay the fish fillets on a large piece of foil; and disperse the pieces of pak choi, chili, ginger, lime zest, and garlic over them. Also, sprinkle the limejuice soy sauce. Now seal the foil paper, leaving enough space inside so that steam is easily circulated. Steam for approximately 15 minutes and serve hot!

Tip: If a steamer is not available, you can gain the same result by putting the seal pack on a heatproof plate that is placed over simmering water.

Thai Lamb

Thai Lamb Stew

Serves 4

This easy stew recipe is made with curry and tomato paste for scrumptious results! Whether you prefer the Indian curry style, or original Southeast-Asian style version of stew, it is perfect to match all tastes. To make it more flavorsome textures, make it with vegetables of your own choice (preferably, eggplant or green beans.

Cooking Time

Total Time: 1 hour and 45 minutes

Prep Time: 45 minutes

Cook Time: 60 minutes

Nutritional value

Calories: 780
Protein: 55g
Fat: 26g
Carbohydrates: 87g
Cholesterol: 145mg

Ingredients

Baby carrots, 2 cups

Bay leaves, 2

Bunch of scallions, 1 (chopped)

Canned beef broth 2-10 ounce

Chopped fennel, 2 cups

Chopped Garlic, 2 tablespoons

Golden raisins, 2 cups

Jasmine Rice (cooked)

Lamb stew meat, 2 lbs

Salt (To taste)

Thai red curry paste, 1 to ounce (Increase or decrease to adjust spices)

Tomato paste, 2 tablespoons

Vegetable oil, 4 tablespoons

Yellow onion, 1 (cut into chunks)

Method

Heat 2 tablespoons of oil in a large pot, and add meat, along with salt for seasoning, until it is brown. To ensure its cooked well, cook it small batches. Then add onions, carrots, garlic, fennel, and red curry paste; and sauté everything for 5 minutes. If required, add some more oil. Next, add in bay leaves, tomato paste, and beef broth and bring the mixture to boil.

Once the meat is tender, add scallions and golden raisins, and cook for another five minutes. Serve hot with plain jasmine rice.

Lamb with Thai Red Curry

Serves 4

If you a true lamb lover, this stir-fried lamb with green apples will leave will your taste buds thanking! Its rich aroma and texture makes it the most desirable Thai lamb entrée.

Cooking Time

Total Time: 35 minutes

Prep Time: 15 minutes

Cook Time: 20 minutes

Nutritional value

Calories: 450
Protein: 27g
Fat: 30g
Carbohydrates: 16g
Cholesterol: 100mg

Ingredients

Chopped onion, 1

Fish sauce, 2 tablespoons

Fresh basil, 1 cup (chopped)

Greens apples, 2 (cut into chunks, unpeeled)

Lamb chunks (precut into bite size pieces) 1 1/4

Minced garlic cloves, 5

Red curry paste, 3 tablespoons

Vegetable oil, 3 tablespoon

Rice noodles or jasmine rice (Optional)

Method

In heated oil, add garlic, onions, and red curry paste. Cook for 3 to 4 minutes. Once the curry is dissolved, add lamb and stir-fry for 7 minutes. Avoid overcooking or the lamb pieces will get very stiff and tough. Now pour in the fish sauce, apples and chopped basil; and cook until all the ingredients are heated through. Serve hot over rice noodles or jasmine rice.

Thai Ginger Lamb on Bamboo Skewers

Serves 4

Love Thai lamb? Do you think it is difficult to make at home? Then you must try this recipe! The world famous lamb is a cinch to cook. The southern Thai dishes have a distinct sweet n sour taste that combines lime with chili Thai sauce.

Cooking Time

Total Time: 4 hours

Prep Time: 3hours, 30 minutes (For preparation and marinade)

Cook Time: 15 minutes

Nutritional value

Calories: 520.8
Protein: 29.6g
Fat: 41.3g
Carbohydrates: 6.2g
Cholesterol: 122.4mg

Ingredients

Brown sugar, 1 tablespoon

Chopped coriander, 2 tablespoons

Chopped ginger, 1 tablespoon

Fish sauce,1 tablespoon

Lamb steaks, 1 1/2 lbs (cut into strips)

Limejuice, 2 tablespoons

Minced garlic cloves, 2

Red chili pepper, 1 (seeded & chopped)

Sesame oil, 3 teaspoons

Sesame seeds, 1 tablespoon

Sweet chili sauce, 2 tablespoons

Steamed jasmine rice

Method

In a bowl, combine lamb strips along with sugar, ginger, fish sauce, sesame oil, and fish sauce and refrigerate for 3 hours. Separately, soak 8 bamboo skewers for half an hour.

Meanwhile, prepare the Thai dipping sauce by combining chili sauce, coriander, and limejuice. Mix well and let it chill in the fridge.

Thread lamb onto the soaked skewers and barbeque each side about 4 to 5 minutes or until meat is completely cooked. Sprinkle over sesame seeds and serve hot with dipping sauce and rice.

Sweet'n'Spicy Thai Lamb Cutlets with Tarragon and Apricot

Serves 4

Cooking Time

Total Time: 3 hours, 25 minutes

Prep Time: 3hours, 15 minutes (For preparation and marinade)

Cook Time: 10 minutes

Nutritional value

Calories: 178.7
Protein: 3.7g
Fat: 7.7g
Carbohydrates: 27.2g
Sugars: 22.5g

Ingredients

Dried apricot, 2/3 cup (chopped)

Honey 2 ½ tablespoons

Hot Thai curry paste, 1 teaspoon

Lamb cutlets, 2 lbs (12 pieces)

Limejuice, 2 teaspoons

Minced tarragon, 2 tablespoons

Olive oil, 2 tablespoons

Salt and black pepper for seasoning

Tarragon sprig for garnishing

Unsalted chicken stock, 2 cups

Method

Marinade apricots in stock along with minced tarragon for 3 hours.

In a food processor, add the apricot marinade, limejuice, salt, pepper, and 1 teaspoon of honey; and pulse until the mixture is smooth. In a small pan, cook the paste for 2 to 3 minutes to heat thoroughly.

Brush the lamb cutlets with a mixture made of curry paste, remaining honey, and oil. Season the meat with salt and pepper according to personal taste. On a preheated gas or charcoal grill, cook the lamb for 5 minutes each side for medium.

Make 4 servings using 3 cutlets on each platter. Dress up with tarragon sprigs and serve hot with apricot sauce.

Thai Lamb Curry

Serves 4

Thailand's street cooking is usually very simple. With minimal amount of basic ingredients, they create the maximum amount of taste. They key is to let the meat marinade for a good time so that the ingredients completely blend into the lamb for a juicy bite.

Cooking Time

Total Time: 1 hour, 30 minutes

Prep Time: 20 minutes

Cook Time: 1 hour, 10 minutes

Nutritional value

Calories: 911.7
Protein: 53.2g
Fat: 66.4g
Carbohydrates: 28.2g
Sugars: 14.7g

Ingredients

Bottled Kaffir lime leaf, 1 teaspoon

Cashew nuts, ½ cup for serving

Chopped lemongrass, 1 stalk

Chopped onion, 1

Coconut cream, 425 g

Diced red capsicum, 1

Grated ginger, 1 teaspoon

Lean lamb, 750 g (cut into small bite-size chunks)

Minced garlic, 2 teaspoons

Thai red curry paste, 2 tablespoons Thai red curry paste

Tomatoes with juice, 425 g

Cooking oil for frying

Method

In a dash of oil, gently fry ginger, garlic, onion, and lemongrass, stirring frequently until the mixture is tender. Carefully stir in lime leaves, curry paste, and stir for 3 minutes. Once it's fragrant, add lamb along with capsicum and tomatoes in juice. Bring the ingredients to boil and lower the heat.

Now pour in the coconut cream, cover the pan and cook for an hour, stirring occasionally. Serve hot over rice with sprinkled cashew nuts.

Thai Lamb Meatballs with Traditional Pita and Yogurt Sauce

Serves 4

This recipe is a lot easier than the traditional Indian kofta with curry, yet tastes even better. Back in homeland, Thailand, It is thought to be one of the most favorite cuisines.

Cooking Time

Total Time: 40 minutes

Prep Time: 20 minutes

Cook Time: 20 minutes

Nutritional value

Calories: 542.9
Protein: 31.2g
Fat: 22.7g
Carbohydrates: 52.8g
Sugars: 8.4g

Ingredients

Chili powder, ½ teaspoon

Cooking spray (olive oil flavored)

Cumin, ½ teaspoon

Diced tomatoes, 2

Egg, 1

Fresh flat parsley leaf, ½ cup

Garlic cloves, 2

Grated ginger, 1 tablespoon

Ground cinnamon, ½ teaspoon

Ground lamb, ½ lb

Ground pepper ¼ teaspoon

Ground turkey, ½ lb

Lightly toasted bread slices, 2

Mint leaves ¼ cup

Pita breads, 4

Quartered onion, 1

Salk, ½ teaspoon

Thai red curry paste, ½ tablespoon

Yogurt Sauce

Chopped fresh dill, 1 tablespoon

Cucumber, 1 (finely diced)

Limejuice, 1 lime

Plain yogurt, 1 cup

Salt and pepper for seasoning

Method

Prepare the Yogurt Sauce

In a bowl, combine all yogurt sauce ingredients and refrigerate to be chilled. Don't forget to season it with salt and pepper before serving.

Prepare the Meatballs

With an oven rack placed in the center, preheat the oven to broil. Spray the cooking oil on a baking sheet.

In a food processor, pulse the bread to make fine crumbs. Then add parsley, cumin, onion, cinnamon, garlic, mint, ginger, chili powder, red curry paste, salt, and pepper; and process until all the ingredients are finely chopped. After transferring the mixture in a bowl, mix in egg followed by adding lamb and turkey. Using hands, mash everything and shape 12 meatballs.

Lightly spray olive oil over the meatballs and place them on the baking sheet prepared earlier. Broil for 20 minutes, turning sides and rotating with the help of a tong.

Once the meatballs are cooked, stuff three meatballs in the center of each pita, and complete its dressing using yogurt sauce and diced tomatoes. Make servings just a few minutes before serving to eat hot!

Thai Curried Lamb with Spiced Up Noodles

Serves 4

Do you have a yen for noodles? Thai national dish never tasted this good before. In 25 minutes, you can treat your senses with a spicy mouthwatering noodle dish with lamb.

Cooking Time

Total Time: 25 minutes

Prep Time: 10 minutes

Cook Time: 15 minutes

Nutritional value

Calories: 525.2
Protein: 29.8g
Fat: 21.5g
Carbohydrates: 56.8g
Sugars: 6.1g
Cholesterol: 37.9mg

Ingredients

Chopped cilantro, 4 tablespoons or Thai basil, 4 tablespoons

Chopped garlic cloves, 2

Chopped green bell pepper , 3/4 cup

Chopped red bell pepper, ¾ cup

Chopped scallions, 2

Cornstarch, 1 teaspoon

Dry sherry, 2 tablespoons dry sherry

Jalapeno chilies, 2 (seeded and chopped)

leg of lamb, 8 ounces (cut into thin strips)

Mild molasses, 1 tablespoon

Oil, 3 tablespoons oil

Peeled chopped ginger, 3 tablespoons

Sambal oelek, 1 teaspoon

Sesame oil, 1 teaspoon

Sliced napa cabbage, 2 cups

Soy sauce, 2 tablespoons

Udan noodles, 8 ounces

Unsweetened coconut milk, 2 tablespoons

Method

Boil Udon noodles as per the directions given on the package, drain, and return to the pan. Add in 1 tablespoon of oil sesame oil and let it rest.

In another bowl, mix sherry and cornstarch until well blended. Then add soy sauce, molasses, coconut milk, and sambal oelek; and set aside.

Heat the remaining 2 tablespoons of oil in a skillet, and add garlic, ginger, chilies, and scallions. After cooking for 2 minutes, add in cabbage, pepper, and lamb and stir-fry until lamb is cooked through. Now pour in the sherry mixture and keep cooking until a thick sauce is formed.

Combine the lamb with boiled noodles and toss over heat to give a good mix.

Sprinkle cilantro over the noodles and serve hot!

Lamp Patties with Thai Dip Sauce

Serves 4

Serve it as a starter or as a main course, it is a perfect choice for all occasions. Planning an outdoor family picnic? It is a party food that is high in both convenience and taste.

Cooking Time

Total Time: 35 minutes

Prep Time: 15 minutes

Cook Time: 20 minutes

Nutritional value

Calories: 525.2
Protein: 29.8g
Fat: 21.5g
Carbohydrates: 56.8g
Sugars: 6.1g
Cholesterol: 37.9mg

Ingredients

Breadcrumbs, 1 cup or Japanese panko breadcrumbs, 1 cup

Chopped coriander, 2 tablespoons

Chopped green onions, 4

Coconut milk, 50 ml

Crushed garlic cloves, 2

Ground lamb, 500g

Limejuice, 1 tablespoon

Olive oil, 2 tablespoons

Red curry paste, 2 tablespoons

Chili sauce

Soy sauce, 3 teaspoons

Sugar, 1 teaspoon

Sweet chili sauce, 2 ½ tablespoons

Water, 2 tablespoons

White wine vinegar, 1 tablespoon

Method

Prepare chili sauce

In a saucepan, combine all chili sauce ingredients and stir until sugar is completely dissolved and a smooth sauce is ready.

Prepare patties

In a large bowl, mix together onion, limejuice, garlic, coconut milk, coriander, breadcrumbs and mince. Make sure you leave some breadcrumbs for dusting before frying. Use your hands to shape the mixture into patties and refrigerate them for 10 minutes. Once the patties are firm, dust the pieces with remaining breadcrumbs and shallow fry until each side is browned and cooked.

Enjoy with sweet and sour chili sauce!

Thai Khao Soi Lamb in Yellow Coconut Curry

Serves 8

Khao Soi is the famous Thai cuisine that is an integral part of the local tradition.

Cooking Time

Total Time: 4 hours, 55 minutes

Marinade: 4 hours

Prep Time: 20 minutes

Cook Time: 35 minutes

Nutritional value

Calories: 628.7
Protein: 3.0g
Fat: 32.5g
Carbohydrates: 85.6g
Sugars: 77.9g

Ingredients

Curry powder, 2 tablespoons

Grape-seed oil, 2 tablespoons

Ground coriander, 2 tablespoons

Ground cumin, 2 tablespoons

Minced garlic cloves, 2

Rack lamb, 1 (with 8 ribs)

Salt (to taste)

Turmeric powder, 1 tablespoon

Kao Soi Curry

Cilantro leaf, 1 cup

Coconut milk, 14 ounce

Curry powder, 1 tablespoon

Fish sauce (to taste)

Ground coriander, 1 tablespoon

Ground cumin, 1 tablespoon

Lime zest, 1

Pickled mustard greens, 1 cup (diced)

Red chili oil, 1 tablespoon

Red curry paste, 4 ounce

Red onion, 1 (diced)

Turmeric powder, ½ tablespoon

Vegetable oil, 2 tablespoons

White sugar (to taste)

Wonton strips, 1 lb

Yellow curry paste, 4 ounce

Method

In a bowl, mix ground coriander seeds, ground cumin, turmeric powder, minced garlic, and curry powder. Rub the mixture of mixed spices over the rack of lamb, place it in a freezer bag, and refrigerate it for 3 to 4 hours. Take it out of the fridge at least half an hour before cooking.

With 2 tablespoons of oil in the pan, cook the curry pastes for 2 to 3 minutes, add on the spices along with coconut cream, and continue cooking for next 5 minutes. Once you see bubbles in the mixture, add fish sauce and sugar to taste and simmer for ½ hour.

Season the lamb with salt, and sear it in a sauté pan greased with grape-seed oil. Once its golden brown, put it in the oven for approximately 18 to 20 minutes. After giving it a rest of 5 minutes, cut the rack into 8 ribs.

Serving

With 2 ounce of wonton noodles in the middle of the platter, place the ribs on top and sprinkle over pickled mustard greens, diced onion, cilantro, and lime zest. Pour the hot curry over the meat, or serve separately.

Spicy Thai Lamb Chops

Serves 4

Cooking Time

Total Time: 30 minutes

Prep Time: 20 minutes

Cook Time: 10 minutes

Nutritional value

Calories: 793.9
Protein: 37.3g
Fat: 68.2g
Cholesterol: 140.6mg
Sugars: 5.0g

Ingredients

Asian fish sauce, 1 tablespoon

Cliantro leaves, 1/3 cup

Garlic cloves, 2

Ketchup, 2 tablespoons

Lamb loin chops, 8 (Each piece about 1" thick)

Limejuice, 1 tablespoon

Peanut oil, 2 tablespoons

Soy sauce, 1 tablespoon

Sugar, 1 teaspoon

Thai green curry paste, 1 tablespoon

Unsalted peanut butter, 1/3 cup

Method

In food processor, make a paste of all ingredients except the meat. Use ¼ portion of paste and spread it over the chops, while mix the remaining ¾ part with 1/3 cup of water.

In a saucepan, cook the mixture of water ingredients paste until a it takes a thick creamy shape.

Grill the chops for 5 minutes each side. Insert an instant read thermometer into the thicket part to check its doneness level. For medium rare, it should record 125 to 130 degrees.

Serve it hot with creamy peanut sauce.

Thai Vegetable

Thai Veg Broth with Coconut Milk

Serves 4

You will find the true aroma of Thailand in this easy to prepare noodle soup.

Cooking Time

Total Time: 25 minutes

Prep Time: 15 minutes

Cook Time: 10 minutes

Nutritional value

Calories: 338
Carbohydrates: 46g
Salt: 1.19g
Protein: 27.4g
Fat: 14g
Saturates: 7g
Sugar: 12g

Ingredients

Thai red curry paste 1½ tablespoon

Vegetable oil 1 teaspoon

Vegetable stock 1liter

Canned coconut milk, 400ml (half fat)

Brown sugar, 2 teaspoon

Medium egg noodles175g

Carrots, 2 (cut into matchsticks)

Sliced Chinese leaf ½ head

Bean sprouts ½ x 300g

Cherry tomatoes, 6 (halved)

Limejuice, 1 Lemon

Finely sliced spring onions, 3

Handful of coriander (roughly chopped)

Method

In a large wok, place the curry paste and fry in oil for about 2 minute. When fragrant, pour in the vegetable stock, brown sugar, and coconut milk; and simmer for 3 to 4 minutes. Now add noodles, Chinese leaf, and carrots and cook until all ingredients are tender. Then mix in tomatoes and bean sprout. Finally, squeeze some lemon along with a bit of seasoning (if you prefer). When serving, sprinkle coriander and spring onions over the broth.

Stir Fried Tofu Thai Pad

Serves 4

Cooking Time

Total Time: 45 minutes

Prep Time: 20 minutes

Cook Time: 25 minutes

Nutritional value

Calories: 270
Carbohydrates: 41
Sodium: 520mg
Protein: 38.8g
Fat: 7g

Ingredients

Pad Thai Sauce, 1-3.25 ounce

Limejuice, 2 tablespoons

Dark brown sugar, 2 tablespoons

Peanut or canola oil for frying

Extra-firm tofu 1-14 ounce (drained)

Chopped onion, 1

Chopped red bell peppers, 1

Minced ginger, 2 tablespoons

Cut baby corn 1-14.4 ounce (drained)

Chopped cilantro ¼ cup

Jasmine Rice (cooked)

Method

In a bowl, whisk pad Thai sauce, sugar, and limejuice until sugar is dissolved.

Then cut the tofu into three slices and place each one in-between a thick paper towel. Dab firmly to absorb any liquid. Now cut each slice into four equal portions (a bite size preferably).

Bring oil to heat and fry the tofu pieces until they are all golden brown. Drain the excess oil and set aside.

With 2 tablespoon oil in the skillet, stir-fry onions, ginger, and red peppers until onions are soft. Then add tofu, pad Thai mixture, and corn until are ingredients are cooked completely. Serve with cooked jasmine rice and cilantro.

Egg plant with Sweet and Spicy Rice Noodles

Serves 4

Cooking Time

Total Time: 45 minutes

Prep Time: 20 minutes

Cook Time: 25 minutes

Nutritional value

Calories: 470
Carbohydrates: 80g
Sodium: 830mg
Protein: 7g
Fat: 15g

Ingredients

Chopped basil, ½ cup

Diced onion, 1

Eggplant, 1 ½ lbs (cut into 1" cubes)

Garlic chili pepper sauce, 3 tablespoons

Limejuice, 2 tablespoons

Minced garlic cloves, 6

Minced ginger, 1 tablespoon

Olive oil, 4 tablespoons

Plum tomatoes, 5 (quartered)

Red bell pepper, 1 (julienned)

Rice Noodles 8 ounce

Salt, 1 teaspoon (or as per your personal taste)

Sweet red chili sauce, 1/3 cup

Method

Boil the noodles and set it aside.

Bring oil to heat in a skillet, and add onions, salt, and eggplant. When the eggplant is browned, add in ginger, garlic, and red bell pepper, ginger and garlic and fry until peppers soften.

Now combine the cooked vegetables with noodles, sweet red chili sauce, plum tomatoes, limejuice, and garlic chili pepper sauce. Add basil when serving!

Grilled Pizza with Thai Peanut Sauce

Serves 1

Cooking Time

Total Time: 30 minutes

Prep Time: 20 minutes

Cook Time: 10 minutes

Nutritional value

Calories: 300
Carbohydrates: 45g
Sodium: 621mg
Protein: 10g
Fat: 3g

Ingredients

Chopped nuts and peanuts, 1 tablespoon

Cooking spray

Fresh cilantro

Italian bread shell 1 8-inch

Mushrooms, 1/2 cup (sliced)

Pea pods, 1/3 cup (sliced)

Peanut sauce, 3 tablespoon

Shredded carrot, 2 tablespoons

Sliced green onion, 2 tablespoons

Method

Preheat the oven to 450°F. On an ungreased baking sheet, place bread shells and bake for about 5 minutes so that its crisp and light brown.

Separately, coat a skillet with cooking, and over medium heat, cook pea pods, mushrooms, and carrots. When all the ingredients are tender, add in green onion.

Spread some peanut sauce over the hot crust. Carefully top it with the cooked vegetables, cilantro, and chopped nuts. Serve hot!

Thai Curried Cauliflower

Serves 4

This authentic Thai vegetarian recipe is a delightful combination of Indian and Thai spices. Both flavors go extremely well with this healthy vegetable. To make it a complete meal, protein is added through chickpeas.

Cooking Time

Total Time: 35 minutes

Prep Time: 20 minutes

Cook Time: 15 minutes

Nutritional value

Calories: 600
Carbohydrates: 107g
Sodium: 1420mg
Protein: 20g
Fat: 12g

Ingredients

Chickpeas, 1-19 ounce

Chopped cilantro, for garnishing

Chopped onions, 2 cups

Diced tomatoes, 1-15

Finely chopped ginger, 1 tablespoon

Finely minced ginger, 1 tablespoon

Frozen Peas, 1-10 ounce

Garlic Chili Pepper Sauce, 1 tablespoon

Oil, 2 tablespoons

Rice Noodles 8 oz

Salt, 1 teaspoon

Small head cauliflower, 1 or 5 cups (broken into florets)

Yellow curry paste, 1 tablespoon

Method

Soak Rice Noodles for sauté.

In boiling salted water, blanch cauliflower for 3 minutes. After draining it, rinse in cold water, and set aside.

In a non-stick pan, bring oil to heat, and sauté ginger, garlic, and onion. Once the ingredients are soft, add tomatoes, garlic chili pepper sauce, salt, and curry paste.

Now stir in drained rice noodles, chickpeas, cauliflower, and peas. Cook until all ingredients are well mixed and rice noodles are completely cooked.

Garnish with cilantro and serve hot!

Creamy Thai Chickpeas

Serves 4

Cooking Time

Total Time: 20 minutes

Prep Time: 10 minutes

Cook Time: 10 minutes

Nutritional value

Calories: 2050
Carbohydrates: 410g
Sodium: 1100mg
Protein: 40g
Fat: 23g

Ingredients

Brown sugar, 1 tablespoon

Chickpeas, 2-15.5 ounce (drained)

Chopped cilantro, 2 tablespoons

Chopped onions, 2 cups

Chopped tomatoes, 1 medium

Coconut milk, 1-13.5 ounce

Cooked Jasmine Rice, 4 cups

Fresh limejuice, 1 tablespoon

Minced garlic cloves, 3

Oil, 2 tablespoons

Soy sauce, 2 tablespoons

Yellow or red curry paste, 1 tablespoon

Method

In a large skillet, bring oil to heat, and over medium heat, cook onions until they start to brown. Then add garlic stir-fry for 2 minutes. Once the garlic is soft, pour in curry paste and ¼ can of coconut milk. As you notice that the curry is dissolved, add the remaining coconut milk, soy sauce, and chickpeas. Bring the mixture to a boil. Now add limejuice, tomatoes, and brown sugar and simmer for 2 minutes.

Sprinkle cilantro over and serve with hot rice!

Thai Veg Delight with Peas and Red Lentils

Serves 4

Nutritional value

Calories: 207
Carbohydrates: 28g
Sugar: 12g
Protein: 10g
Fat: 7g

Cooking Time

Total Time: 45 minutes

Prep Time: 10 minutes

Cook Time: 35 minutes

Ingredients

Baby spinach, 100g (roughly chopped)

Brown basmati rice (to server)

Chopped onions, 2

Diced aubergine (eggplant), 1

Frozen peas, 140g

Low sodium vegetable stock, 500ml

Mango chutney (to serve)

Red lentils, 75g

Red or yellow peppers, 2 (deseeded and cut into wedges)

Red Thai curry paste, 1 or 2 tablespoons (depending on the preferred taste)

Reduced fat coconut milk, 200ml

Method

In a non-stick pan, heat the curry paste with a splash of the stock. Now add the chopped onions and cook until they have softened. Gently stir in aubergine. Add in more stock if it starts to stick to the pan. After 5 minutes, add in coconut milk, lentil, peppers, and the remaining stock and cook for another 15 minutes.

Then pour in the frozen peas and spinach. Turn off the stove one spinach is wilted. Serve hot with mango chutney and rice.

Thai Pineapple Curry with Squash

Serves 4

Nutritional value

Calories: 207
Carbohydrates: 28g
Sugar: 12g
Protein: 10g
Fat: 7g

Cooking Time

Total Time: 40 minutes

Prep Time: 10 minutes

Cook Time: 30 minutes

Ingredients

Chopped coriander leaves (to add and to garnish)

Chopped onion, 1

Frozen green beans, 140g

Medium butternut squash, 500g/1lb 2oz (peeled, deseeded and cut into chunks)

Pineapple chunks, 237g

Reduced fat coconut milk, ½ x 400ml

Sunflower or vegetable oil, 1 tablespoon

Thai red curry paste, 4 teaspoons

Vegetable stock, 200ml

Method

Fry the onions in a heated wok for 5 minutes. Once softened, pour in the red curry paste along with stock and coconut milk. Simmer until the squash is tender (approximately for 15 to 20 minutes). Then tip in green beans and stir for two minutes. Now add coriander and pineapple and cook until everything is heated thoroughly.

Sprinkle over coriander leaves and serve with hot noodles and rice.

Veggie Thai Tofu with Mushrooms

Serves 4

This fragrant Thai veggie dish will get your taste buds into action. Thai cuisines are usually very complex; however, this will make things easier. Under one hour, you can prepare the most mouthwatering veggie main course.

Nutritional value

Calories: 233
Carbohydrates: 11g
Sugar: 7g
Protein: 8g
Fat: 18g

Cooking Time

Total Time: 50 minutes

Prep Time: 20 minutes

Cook Time: 30 minutes

Ingredients

Aubergine, 1 (chopped into chunks)

Basil (leaves picked), 20g

Brown sugar, 1 teaspoon

Chopped red pepper, ½ (deseeded)

Cooked jasmine rice (to serve)

Courgette, 1 (chopped into chunks)

Cubed tofu, 200g

Lime juice, 3 limes

Mushrooms, 140g mushrooms

Red chilies, 2 (1 sliced into rounds, 1 chopped)

Reduced fat coconut milk, 400ml

Soy sauce, 4 to 5tablespoons

Sugar snap peas, 140g

Vegetable oil, 2 tablespoon

For the paste

Chopped lemongrass, 1

Chopped red pepper, ½ red pepper (deseeded)

Chopped shallots, 3

Coriander stalks, 20g

Freshly ground pepper, 1 teaspoon

Garlic cloves, 2

Grated ginger, (thumb-sized)

Ground coriander, 1 teaspoon

Lime zest, 1 lime

Red chilies, 3

Method

Combine all the paste ingredients in a food processor and pulse until well mixed. Marinate the tofu in lime juice, chopped chili, and soy sauce.

Heat 1 tablespoon of oil in a pan and fry 2 tablespoons of paste for 2 minutes. Pour in 100ml water along with coconut milk. Then add aubergine, pepper, and courgette, and cook until almost tender.

In the remaining oil, fry the drained tofu until golden.

Add all mushroom, basil and sugar snaps to the curry. Season it with lime juice, sugar, and soy sauce. Cook the mixture for approximately 5 minutes, or until mushrooms are tender. Now add tofu and heat through.

Garnish it with basil and sliced chili. Serve with hot jasmine rice for a divine taste.

Traditional Tofu in Thai Orange Sauce

Serves 4

With this easy-to-follow recipe, everyone can enjoy the fantastic flavors of Thai cuisine. You do not even have to pay a trip to the Asian spice shop, as the ingredients can easily be found in your local grocery store.

Nutritional value

Calories: 330
Carbohydrates: 28g
Sodium: 280mg
Protein: 15g
Fat: 18g

Cooking Time
Total Time: 30 minutes

Ingredients

Canola oil, 2 tablespoons

Cherry tomatoes, 1 cup (halved)

Firm tofu, 1lb, or 453.5g

Orange juice, 1 cup

Peanut Sauce Mix, 3 ounce

Scallions, 1 bunch

Cooked Jasmine Rice or Rice Noodles (Optional, for serving)

Method

Cut drained tofu into 3 slices. Using a paper towel, pat the tofu firmly until the water is completely absorbed. Now divide each slice into 4 bite size pieces.

In a preheated pan, fry the tofu pieces, turning each side, until they are golden brown. Pat with a paper towel to remove oil.

Separately, slice green onions (scallions) into thin rounds. You can reserve the dark green part for garnishing. Add this to the same skillet and stir-fry for 2 minutes. Now carefully pour in peanut sauce mix and orange juice, and the mixture to boil. Turn the heat down and simmer for another two minutes. Once the sauce has a smooth texture, add tomatoes and fried tofu and cook until all ingredients are heated through.

Garnish it with dark green part of green onions, and serve hot with jasmine rice or rice noodles.

Conclusion

This cookbook has compiled 50 versatile Thai cuisines that focus on time saving and easy to find ingredients. East has to offer a special taste their traditional spices and ingredients that are an integral part of their food culture. As much as Americans like their food, they usually find it difficult to cook Thai dishes.

However, when you have this book with you, you need not to order a home delivery or take away even for your midnight cravings. Whether you are in mood for some healthy eating that combines various vegetables, or have the hunger for juicy meat with a creamy sauce, this book has it all in the palm of your hands.

23409729R00056

Printed in Great Britain
by Amazon